HOPE HAPPENS!

CATHERINE DeVRYE

HOPε HAPPεNS!

WORDS OF ENCOURAGEMENT
FOR TIMES OF CHANGE

POCKET BOOKS

New York   London   Toronto   Sydney   Singapore

Photo credits
Photos on pages 46 and 76 were taken by the author's father, Hendrick DeVrye. All other photos except that on page 1 were taken by the author, Catherine DeVrye. The photos represent every continent, symbolic of the universal human spirit.

POCKET BOOKS, a division of Simon & Schuster, Inc.
1230 Avenue of the Americas, New York, NY 10020

Originally published in Australia in 2002 by Everest Press

ISBN: 0-7434-7627-1

First Pocket Books trade paperback edition June 2003

10 9 8 7 6 5 4 3 2 1

POCKET and colophon are registered trademarks of Simon & Schuster, Inc.

Manufactured in the United States of America

For information regarding special discounts for bulk purchases, please contact Simon & Schuster Special Sales at 1-800-456-6798 or business@simonandschuster.com

For my parents...and every parent and child
who ever loved or was loved...

For my grandparents, aunts, uncles and
friends...and for all of yours...

For those dedicated professionals and
volunteers who daily offer hope and help to
others facing seemingly hopeless situations.

Introduction

I sat in the lounge of Brisbane Airport on September 11, 2001, having just addressed the World Airline Entertainment Association. I felt incredibly sad and numb, not just because of global events but, somewhat selfishly, because of bronchitis and a relationship with the man of my dreams threatening to turn into a nightmare. It hadn't just been 'one of those days' but one of those weeks, when a lot of things in my little part of the world weren't going according to plan (at least, not to my plan!)

A friend phoned to say her mother had died. Certainly, she shared compassion with thousands of people on the other side of the world, but the loss of one life weighed far heavier on her mind. To her, talk of the 'world changing' was more than a media cliché about the world changing—the world always changes—but her own life had tumbled and changed irrevocably with the death of the one person who had always been central to her world.

I couldn't help but think that, undoubtedly, global tragedy impacts on us all in various ways, from the personal to the economic. Yet, ultimately, it's the everyday tragedies in life that cause us the greatest grief, wherever we live on the globe.

My thoughts were interrupted by a vibrant young woman, who introduced herself and said she had been inspired by one of my presentations some years ago. She went on to say that she'd since been promoted to London and took only six books overseas...one being the last one I'd written, *Hot Lemon & Honey— Reflections for Success in Times of Change*.

'Whenever I'm feeling despondent, I delve into that book and magically find just the right words of inspiration and encouragement,' she enthused.

'Oh, what chapter was that?' I asked, before smiling at the irony.

The young woman had lifted my spirits. But, despite her claim that my book was her source of encouragement and inspiration, I personally don't believe that any one person can motivate any other, and that inspiration and encouragement come from a variety of sources—in the least expected forms, from the most unlikely people, in the most peculiar places.

I am often concerned when, after I address a room full of people, some audience members exclaim in a well-meaning way: 'You changed my life today!'

Although these comments are offered in the most complimentary vein, I'm troubled that a total stranger can think that a few words from me, or anyone else, can change his or her life. Admittedly, it's wonderful to have countless letters and emails from readers or conference attendees, stating that some words I'd written or spoken have helped them. Comments range from crediting me with 'improving productivity 40%' in a multinational corporation to 'mending a broken teenage romance'...not that I consider myself an 'expert' in either field.

I do feel truly blessed in my work and, although I would love to think that I was able to help to that extent, I'm also realistic enough to know that nothing I said actually made those differences. The impact was made by what those individuals heard. More so, it was what they *chose* to hear at that point in time, and what they then decided to *act* upon. My words simply served as a timely catalyst for change.

Therefore, it is not surprising that I have a low tolerance for so-called gurus who claim they 'change people's lives'. No one can change the life of any individual except that individual. Certainly, others offer a greater or lesser incentive for a person to improve his or her life. Nonetheless, responsibility still rests with each one of us for our own lives!

Recently I received an email stating: 'Thanks. You kick-started my belief system again.'

This particular communication resonated more with me because we have all had times in our lives when our belief systems needed a good kick-start, and words of others can help in that regard.

You may have already heard some of the quotes in this book. Others, you will not have heard. Some may not resonate with you at the moment. Others may never do so. Some may have deep meaning. Others may have none. But there may be one that means a lot and can help you cope with your lot in life.

I've collected motivational quotes, poems and stories since my grandfather died when I was sixteen. As I was an only child, he had been my confidante and best friend and when my parents passed away a few years later, I re-visited those initial inscriptions in my diary and have since added to them over the years.

People often asked how I coped when my folks died when I was 21? What choice did I have? Cope or crumble—and, I had no intention of crumbling. Sure, there have been many crumbled days of despair since then but I've always tried to remember what Frank Jansen, a wise old man, told me when I first arrived in Australia:

'Cath...Every day above the ground is a good one.'

This was one of the first statements that made any sense to me, when nothing else did.

Because I experienced loss at an early age and *felt* I had no one else to turn to, I turned inward—to myself and to books. Two university friends gave me the first two 'motivational' books in my library and, years later, these books are still there, although more dog-eared with now yellowing pages.

I've subsequently added many such books to my library, quickly discarded others and even written a couple myself. I've highlighted particular paragraphs that meant something to me at the time of reading and, at times, when I'm temporarily feeling despondent, I may reach for a book, to re-read a particular page. Some sentences and sentiments have made such impact that I've occasionally copied the words from inside the pages of a book to place prominently on the outside of my fridge, or on my bathroom mirror, desk or bedside table, as every-day reminders.

Even though I had not lost any loved ones on September 11, 2001 and it had been over a quarter of a century since my parents passed away, I felt a strangely similar sense of disbelief and sadness. So, once again I turned to the pages of my diary, searching for words of encouragement and scribbling some thoughts. Before I knew it, I was gathering them into this little book—to hopefully help others work through their tough times, faster than I did mine.

Since those early dark days, I've been privileged to meet world leaders, sports stars and music icons and have been surprised to discover that, at times, they all share the same sense of loss and uncertainty as my next-door neighbour or a stranger on a bus, train or plane. Behind the facade, no life is perfect and the grass isn't always greener on the other side of the fence.

So, when we wallow in self-pity, it's important to remember that there is almost always someone much worse off than ourself.

Tragedy strikes all of us sooner or later. In my case, it just happened to be sooner than some. So, I've written this book for the everyday person with everyday problems in this journey called life. And, we're all everyday people! As John Lennon once said: 'Life is what happens when we're making other plans.' Today, and every day, we need to keep our plans and our dreams alive and must not be swamped by nightmares of negativity and despair.

Hope is no magical panacea to problems we face, but hope helps us cope when the well is dry of wishes. One can only have courage if one has hope. We need both in tough times.

There will, of course, be times when, unfortunately, no amount of optimism can change the situation. Soon after the first release of this book, a friend's son died. My friend and his family never appeared to lose hope throughout his son's illness and I was lost for adequate words of sympathy.

I knew from my own experience that, immediately after the loss of a loved one, loss of health, loss of wealth or loss of a job, no words from anyone else can help a lot in the short term. But, over time, a lot of little words can help a little—*if* you let them.

Surprisingly, it is the simplest homespun truths that are the ones that stand us in good stead in times of strife. I trust that some of the quotes in this book will be both timely and timeless on your journey; acting as a turning point when you've hit a low point.

Friends know and appreciate that my life has had as many ups and downs as any. Heartfelt thanks to them for their support over the years—especially the handful whose counsel I sought on this book and to the terrific behind the scenes publishing team—none of whom ever lost hope in the concept.

American humourist, Art Buchwald, once said:

'Whether it's the best of times or the worst of times, it's the only time we have.'

Let's make every moment count, starting now. Someone once accused me of being overly optimistic and living my life by clichés. If that's the opposite of being overly negative and not living one's life to the full, I plead guilty—and you can quote me on that!

Catherine DeVrye

There are always
more **choices** than
you think.

Catherine DeVrye

What lies behind us and
what lies before us are but
small matters compared to
what lies **within** us.

Ralph Waldo Emerson

Out of difficulties
grow miracles.

Jean De La Bruyere

Light always
follows darkness.

Anonymous

There are only two ways
to live your life.
One is as though nothing
is a miracle.
The other is as though
everything is a miracle.

Albert Einstein

Yesterday's history.

Tomorrow's a mystery.

All we have is today and

it's called the present

because it's a

precious gift.

Anonymous

15

Life is either
a daring adventure
or nothing.

Helen Keller

In the midst of winter
I finally learned that
there was in me an
invincible summer.

Albert Camus

Your pain is the

breaking of the shell that

encloses your

understanding.

Kahlil Gibran

What the caterpillar calls the end, the rest of the world calls a butterfly.

Lao Tsu

Do not compare yourself with others. You may become vain and bitter; for always there will be greater and lesser persons than yourself...

...Be yourself. Especially, do not feign affection. Neither be cynical about love; for in the face of all aridity and disenchantment it is as perennial as the grass...

Excerpts from 'Desiderata'

21

We cannot **discover** new oceans until we have the **courage** to lose sight of the shore.

Gide

The greatest discovery
of my generation is
that a human being can
alter his life by altering
his attitude.

William James

Of all the people you will know in a lifetime, you are the only one you will never leave nor lose. To the question of your life, you are the only answer. To the problems in your life, you are the only solution.

Anonymous

When a door closes...
look for an **open** window...
but it may take a while
to feel the breeze.

Anonymous

You may have to fight
a battle more than once
to **win** it.

Margaret Thatcher

Being defeated is often a
temporary condition.
Giving up is what
makes it permanent.

Marilyn Vos Savant

Whatever our country by birth
  or by choice,
Now is the time to unite with
  one voice.
As we look to the future with
  respect for the past,
And strive in the present for
  dreams that will last,

To reach our potential as one
 and a nation,
Giving all a fair go without
 hesitation.
And regardless of faith, to
 keep faith...
in our future, our planet and
 ourself.

Catherine DeVrye

When you get to
the end of your rope,
tie a knot
and **hang on.**

Franklin D. Roosevelt

Courageous men
never lose the zest for
living even though their
life situation is zestless.

Martin Luther King Jr

One who wants
a rose must respect
the thorn.

Persian proverb

Life is what happens when we're making other plans.

John Lennon

34

The poor man is not
he who is without a cent
but he who is without
a dream.

Harry Kemp

If I had my life to live over,
I would perhaps
have more actual troubles
but fewer imaginary ones,
eat more ice cream and
less beans.

Harold Kushner

Only one principle
will give you courage—
that is the principle
that no evil lasts forever
nor indeed for very long.

Epicurus, 271 BC

Be where you are—
otherwise you will miss
your life.

Buddha

Regret for things we did
can be tempered by time;
it is regret for the things
we did not do
that is inconsolable.

Sydney J. Harris

Whether you believe
you can or you believe
you can't—you're right
either way.

Henry Ford

Belief in ourselves
is like a muscle—it is
strengthened by
constant and careful use.

Catherine DeVrye

41

It's not the mountain
we conquer but
ourselves.

Sir Edmund Hillary

Grant that I may be given
appropriate difficulties and
sufferings on this journey
so that my heart might be
truly awakened and my
practice of universal liberation
and compassion may
be truly fulfilled.

Tibetan prayer

If you can keep your head
  when all about you are
  losing theirs and blaming it
  on you;
If you can trust yourself when
  all men doubt you, and
  make allowance for their
  doubting too.

If you can wait and not be
tired of waiting, or being
lied about, don't deal in lies,
or being hated don't give
way to hating and yet don't
look too good, nor talk
too wise...

Rudyard Kipling

45

If you **travel** a path without obstacles, it probably doesn't lead anywhere.

Catherine DeVrye

Don't look back unless you plan to go that way.

Anonymous

Reflect upon
your blessings,
of which every man
has plenty, not on your
past misfortunes, of which
all men have some.

Charles Dickens

You can't drive into the **future** if you're **looking** into a rear vision mirror.

Catherine DeVrye

Not everything that is faced can be **changed** but nothing can be changed until it is faced.

James Baldwin

What would you

attempt to do

if you knew

you could not fail?

Dr Robert Schuller

The most difficult matter is
not so much to change
the world as yourself.

Nelson Mandela

Tough times don't last—
tough people **do**.

Anonymous

The **only** thing
we have to fear
is fear itself.

Franklin D. Roosevelt

54

Things work out best
for people who make
the best of the way
things work out.

John Wooden

Count your blessings—

not your troubles.

Dad (Hendrick DeVrye)

Learn your lessons quickly—and move on.

Eileen Caddy

In times like these, it is good to remember that there have always been times like these.

Paul Harvey

Nothing endures forever.
Everything perishes in time.
So laugh and love while
   you may,
Help who you can—work
   while you must
And when the end comes
   so be it.
All fame ends in oblivion and
   is soon forgotten

But it is fun to strive, joy
    to win.
It is a challenge to lose and
    try again
And victory always comes if
    you try hard enough.
To lose is not to fail.
The only failure is to lose and
    not try again.

Anonymous

Cross your **bridges**
when you come to them—
or you pay the toll twice.

Mum (Margaret Miller Gallacher Smart)

The pessimist sees the
difficulty in every opportunity.
The optimist,
the opportunity in
every difficulty.

L. P. Jacks

...Two things stand like stone,
kindness in
another's troubles,
and courage in one's own.

Adam Lindsay Gordon

Find **courage**

in dis-courage-ment.

Catherine DeVrye

I do not wish you joy without
 a sorrow,
Nor endless day without the
 healing dark,
Nor brilliant sun without the
 restful shadows,
Nor tides that never turn
 against your barque.

I wish you love and faith and
strength and wisdom.
Goods, gold enough to help
some needy one.
I wish you songs but also
blessed silence
And God's sweet peace when
every day is done.

Dorothy Nell McDonald

To **dream** of the person you would like to be is to waste the person **you are**.

Anonymous

God grant me the
serenity to accept the
things I cannot change;
the courage to change
the things I can and
the wisdom to know
the difference.

Anonymous

Never give in.
Never. Never. **Never**.
Never.

Winston Churchill

Whether it is the **best** of times or the worst of times, it is the **only** time you've got.

Art Buchwald

Don't ask for
an easier life. Ask to be
a stronger person.

Anonymous

If all people were to bring their miseries together in one place, most would be glad to take, each, their own home again—rather than take a portion out of the common stock.

Solon, 559 BC

There are **no** hopeless
situations. There are only men
who have grown hopeless
about them.

Clare Booth Luce

A **smile** is a frown **turned** upside down.

Granddad (David Smart)

It's OK to be down in
the dumps—just don't stay
there too long.

Catherine DeVrye

We may encounter
many defeats
but we must not
be defeated.

Maya Angelou

No man fails
who **does** his **best**.

Orison Swett Marden

There is
no **education**
like adversity.

Benjamin Disraeli

We are all in the gutter

but some of us are

looking at the stars.

Oscar Wilde

The hero is no braver
than an ordinary man—
but he is brave
five minutes longer.

Ralph Waldo Emerson

Never bear more than one
kind of trouble at a time.
Some people bear three—
all they have had,
all they have now and
all they expect to have.

Edward Hale

Inside myself is a place where I live alone and that's where you **renew** your **spring** that **never** dries up.

Pearl Buck

Men are born
to succeed not to fail.

Henry David Thoreau

Our fears are more
numerous than our dangers
and we suffer more in
our imagination
than reality.

Seneca

May you live all the days
of your life.

Jonathan Swift

Create your tomorrows with your thoughts and actions today.

Catherine DeVrye

Find purpose—
the means will follow.

A billboard somewhere in India

The great danger
for most of us is not that
our aim is too high
and we miss,
but that it is too low and
we achieve it.

Michelangelo

Every day **above** the ground is a **good** one!

Frank Jansen

'I **tried** and it didn't work'
is a **lot better** than
'I wish I'd tried'.

Anonymous

There are no failures—
only learners.

Buckminster Fuller

If there were no clouds

we should not

enjoy the sun.

Proverb

If you want
the rainbow,
you gotta put up
with the rain.

Dolly Parton

Fall seven times.
Stand up eight.

Japanese proverb

Pick yourself up when
you're feeling down.
No one else is likely to.

Catherine DeVrye

Nothing in life is to
be feared. It is only to be
understood.

Marie Curie

Fear is **never** a reason for quitting.
It is **only** an excuse.

Norman Vincent Peale

If you can't find your **way** out of any difficulty, it's probably because you're **looking** for an easy way out.

Anonymous

Everything that is
done in the world
is done by hope.

Martin Luther King

We are disturbed
not by things that happen
but by our opinion of the
things that happen.

Epictetus

Experience is not
what happens to you.
It is what **you do** with
what happens to you.

Aldous Huxley

Keep your face to the **sunshine** and you cannot see the shadows.

Helen Keller

Each player must accept
the cards life deals him or her.
But once they are in hand, he
or she alone must decide
how to play the cards
in order to win the game.

Voltaire

No one ever damaged their
eyesight looking on the
brighter side of life.

Anonymous

It is not because things
are difficult that we
do not **dare**; it is because
we do not dare
that they are difficult.

Seneca

Don't be afraid
your **life** will end—be afraid
it will never **begin**.

Grace Hansen

Every substantial grief
has 20 shadows and most
of the shadows are of
your own making.

Sydney Smith

Be realistic.
Plan for a miracle.

Bhagwan Shree Rajneesh

I was taught that
the way of **progress** is
neither swift nor easy.

Madame Curie

Life is not the way it's
supposed to be.
It's the way it is. The way
you cope with it is what
makes the difference.

Virginia Satir

Hope Happens!

Hope is what happens when you first
    see a light
Just a distant, small star in the darkest
    of night.

Hope is what happens with the first buds
    of spring
When dawn touches the sky or a bird
    spreads it's wings.

Hope is what happens when a wound
    starts to heal
Whether skin deep or soul deep, you begin
    to feel real.

Hope is what happens when you're poor
    but not broken
There's a goldmine of dreams — just not
    yet awoken.

Hope is what happens when someone
    is kind
A feeling not lost—just misplaced in
    your mind.

Hope is what happens when war turns
    to peace
After everyone prayed that the fighting
    would cease.

Hope is what happens with the smell of
 fresh rain
When your long drought of dreams is
 renewed yet again.

Hope is what happens when clouds
 finally clear
Troubled thunder falls silent—courageous
 whispers you hear.

Hope is what happens when your heart
 skips a beat
And, so least expected, a soul mate
 you meet.

Hope is what happens when fresh bread
 is baking
And what hungers your heart, will one day
 stop aching.

hope

Hope is what happens when kindling ignites
You rediscover your passion that burns day
    and night.

Hope is what happens when the pain eases
    a bit
And deep down inside, you find your
    true grit.

Hope is what happens as long as we breathe
For although it takes time, the sorrow
    will leave.

Hope is what happens long after the pain
Hope is what happens — again and again.

Catherine DeVrye

happen

Yes...Hope happens!

If you need some hope happening in your life at the moment, or in the future, open any page at random and you'll be surprised that whatever message you read may be most pertinent at the time.

It's no coincidence that this book is in your hands. I hope it helps because your life is also in your hands and...hope can truly happen, if you let it!

Catherine DeVrye

Photographic credits

Hope Happens! contains an image from every continent on Earth, symbolic of the universal human spirit, regardless of race, religion or geographic location. All but three were taken by the author. Her original color negatives have been transposed into monotone. The images on pages 46 and 76 were taken by the author's father, Hendrick DeVrye and the one on page 1 by Justin Thomas.

Please visit the author's website at
www.greatmotivation.com or contact her at
books@greatmotivation.com